LADY SIDEKICK

LADY SIDEKICK

50 TIRED TROPES FOR WOMEN

ANNEKA HARRY
ILLUSTRATED BY LAURA DOCKRILL

The
History
Press

Anneka Harry is a writer and performer whose work covers series, episodes and features for the likes of the BBC, Channel 4, ITV2, Radio 4, *Stylist* and *Grazia*. Her first book *Gender Rebels: 50 Influential Cross-Dressers, Impersonators, Name-Changers and Game-Changers* was published by Little A in 2020.

First published 2020

The History Press
97 St George's Place, Cheltenham,
Gloucestershire, GL50 3QB
www.thehistorypress.co.uk

British Library Cataloguing in Publication Data.
A catalogue record for this book is available from the British Library.

ISBN 978 0 7509 9525 2

Typesetting and origination by The History Press
Printed in Turkey by Imak

CONTENTS

INTRODUCTION

The gender inequality on our screens and across popular culture is so grim it's sporting a hooded cloak and clutching a scythe. Women and girls are a mega-ton more than the 2D versions we constantly see portrayed and its ripple effect has got us wading through misogyny-flavoured treacle (if you think that sounds in the least bit appetising, you're a stonking great bazonga-gawking sexist – *away with ya!*).

We need less censorship of female behaviour. We need more women and we need *raw* women. We need not for personalities to be depicted by skin or hair colour alone. We need for women to stop being used as props or reduced to slabs. We need to say buh-bye to binaries, to mythical beauty standards and to being 'nice'. We need plots that don't revolve solely around women's rape, exploitation and/or death. We need women to no longer be outnumbered by penises or have been written only to have one symbolically, or in actuality, thrust toward her. We need to go back to basics and bust apart the dead horse female character tropes the industry is still tirelessly trotting out and incessantly flogging. It goes without saying that male tropes suck too, but the majority have had guys feeling like they can unremittingly swing stuff their way since forever ago (and just look where that's got us). Sadly, there's a batrillion more from whence these came and new tropes are rearing their repellent heads on a daily basis.

Lady Sidekick has been created with a mind to elevate and disrupt; I hope you are compelled to rip out, laminate, frame or take a highlighter to every page (and you may find that it pairs very nicely with an industrial vat of wine). The case studies are twisted and oversimplified representations because tropes are meant to depower and dehumanise women. If any of the language, terminology or illustrations doth offend, spike your blood pressure or ruin your enjoyment of this book, then please remember that it's *sort of the point*...

Until we can laugh at the mess we're in, we'll never get out of it.

This book is dedicated to my Knight in Shining Armour, Lizzie Brown.

Thank you to my gang of Lauras for making this happen, with special mention to my (non-tropey) Funny BFF, Laura Dockrill. You've brought these women to life and you bring pure joy to mine. Long may we raise and save each other.

I would also like to acknowledge myself (so sue me). I wrote *Lady Sidekick* in the midst of all manner of personal and global life-changing madness. It will forever remind me of my own hero-character strength. Reader, I hope you know yours.

THE

TROPES

THE BEAUTIFUL ALL ALONG BABE

How did we not notice that behind the orthodontic headgear, the world's most bangable woman was patiently awaiting a glow-up and rhetoric rebrand? We had an inkling her interest in everything other than being an object must have been a cover-up. We feel so silly now!

'She's never been kissed because she reads ... but THE BEAUTIFUL ALL ALONG BABE's juice was always slyly worth the squeeze!'

(Just cut to the bit where she washes her hair and gets laser eye surgery. Save yourself two hours.)

THE BIMBO

On Wednesdays she wears pink (and on Mondays, Tuesdays, Thursdays, Fridays, Saturdays and Sundays). She's stupid but stunning and her Daddy's rich. Now, somebody find her a 'gorgey-gorge' guy to adore, quick! (Before she starts talking and ruining the view.)

@the_girl_next_door wow hunni bunni so beaut

@partygirlofficial YAAS BISH! Werk it! #WeNeedToGoDancing #ShotsSoon

@footiefreddie daaaamn girl

@garygunsandgains 12/10

@beerzandbirdz •• 🤙 💯

@jackthelad69 Fellas, stay clear! Trusss me. The only good thing about dating her woz her mum's a MILF 😂😂😂 I've never met any1 in my life who *actually* says 'XOXO'! Or any1 who needs an emotional support micro pig for that matter 🐷🐷🐷 Nah man. I'm not pretending to be Stephen Hawkings out here but THIS GIRL KILLS CACTUS! Duh. Vocab of a fridge magnet, bruv! Honestly, don't fall for it! She'll try and communicate with u in teacup yorkshire terrier GIFs and make u build bare shelves in her shoe cupboard. Yeah yeah, she's buff ... but she gets an entire makeup team in for 3hrs and then calls it her '5-minute look'! 💅 I'm DEAD. Do yourself a favour lads ... RUN! 🏃💨 #DumbAsRocks #BIMBO

THE BRATTY TEENAGE DAUGHTER

No dysfunctional family would be complete without a mood-swinging, septum-piercing drama queen. If she's not acting out for attention, you better believe it's because she's been told her boyfriend can't stay the night (and take the virginity her parents still think she possesses).

If you answer 'Yes' to one or more of these questions, then you have yourself a BRATTY TEENAGE DAUGHTER. Congratulations!

★ If there's a storm, would her gob be the eye of it?
★ Has she reached 'max' on the faux outrage barometer?
★ Is she only attracted to plug sockets in coffee shops and bad boys who play air drums with utensils?
★ Did she drop out of school to devote her life to door slamming?
★ Is her ego so big she beeps when she walks backwards?
★ Does it feel like only yesterday she was enjoying 'tummy time' and now you're resisting the urge to punch her in the throat?
★ Is she currently negotiating an ill-advised green balayage hair phase?
★ Does she require a JCB to remove her head from her backside?
★ Is she sponsored by PMS?

N.B. If you have a badly behaved teenage *son*, worry not! He is 'spirited' at worst and exceptional at best.

THE BRIDEZILLA

Imagine a monster in bridal couture, waterboarding the florist and impaling her caterers with their own skewers — you've got BRIDEZILLA! She may be a Super Trope, but this bride has zilch super powers (unless you include being a self-centered, satanic, control-freak maniac).

Your invitation
to the wedding of all millennia

Bridezilla and Some Pitiful Sod or Other
request the pleasure of your monetary gifts and jealousy
at their eye-bulgingly expensive wedding,
which *Bridezilla*, being constitutionally incapable
of compromise, has singlehandedly micro-managed via
Pinterest and order-barking.

Although *Bridezilla* has a toddler's arrogance, the
couple unfortunately cannot accommodate children.
Bridezilla's wedding will be better than yours and
her children will be too (once the big day is done and she
instantaneously becomes PREGZILLA).
Motherhood may be a woman's greatest goal but, due to
unforeseen circumstances, *Bridezilla*'s 'best friend' will
no longer be permitted to join the bridal party, as she's given
birth and gained a chin.

Guests are kindly asked to share their photos of the day
with the hashtag provided, and if *Bridezilla* doesn't get
enough likes, she'll file for divorce. This is about a dress not
happily ever after.

RSVP IMMEDIATELY
#TheMostDazzlingBrideInTheWorld

THE BUTCH LESBIAN

No need to panic, we haven't let a man slip onto the list! We know that butch women are the least palatable of all the women so feel free to skip this section if you're feeling unwell. All that feminazi-ing and fanny chasing is as nauseating as her handlebar moustachioed chops ...

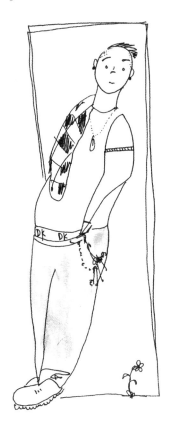

BUTCH BASICS 101:

- ✔ Gold-star lesbian (THE HEAD OF ALL LESBIANS)
- ✔ Aggressively short
- ✔ Proportionally effed-up shoulder bulk
- ✔ Breath so hot it could mull wine
- ✔ Talks smack about men for a living
- ✔ Out to steal your wife
- ✔ Angry about always being excluded and so makes a point of speaking out about it. See also: men on International Women's Day
- ✔ Dadbod
- ✔ Tash rash
- ✔ Opens beer bottles with lighters
- ✔ Carabiner with more keys than a caretaker
- ✔ Radiates Big Lesbian Energy and body odour
- ✔ Buzzcut (obviously)
- ✔ Flannel shirt (obviously)
- ✔ Baggy jeans (obviously)
- ✔ Boxers (obviously)
- ✔ Gravedigger boots (obviously)
- ✔ Thumb ring (obviously)
- ✔ The Man in the relationship (obviously)
- ✔ Continually pushing a Gaygenda™
- ✔ Subaru owner
- ✔ Boot full of camping equipment
- ✔ On the prowl for adorable blonde prey to recruit
- ✔ Never does as a gay go by without mention of THE BUTCH LESBIAN's gayness

THE CAT LADY

She'll doubtless be single from womb to tomb so she's dating a bunch of flea-ridden felines instead! Frequently mistaken for THE BAG LADY (same same but different) she screams and shakes her fists for a living because she's manless and therefore MAD.

FREAKS OF NATURE
WELCOMES ITS LATEST CAST MEMBER

ROLL UP! ROLL UP!
And witness THE CAT LADY with your very eyes!

She's antique (over forty), follicly challenged, about as appealing as a series of laminated food photos in a cafe window and she lives with eighty-five mangy cats!

You've heard of a forehead ... this woman has a fivehead! Once you've seen the barren spinster for yourself, she can never be unseen! This charm vacuum has no past life worth mentioning, she's been on a lifetime sex drought, uses a flap-front phone case and (like all the other unattractive women who have gone before her) she wears long-sleeved pyjamas!

Today, for one day only, we are offering a rare sighting of THE CAT LADY, in the flesh. She's worn her favourite 'THE END IS NIGH' sandwich board just for you! Don't be scared folks, she's not on glue, she's high on kitty litter! And the most unbelievable part of all? Her cats *actually choose* to live with her!

What's that I hear you cry? CAT LADIES are prejudiced tropes? Nonsense! Men can own cats too ... but they'd be Cat BACHELORS! This is a freakshow not a dating agency!

THE CLUMSY COSPLAY OTAKU GIRL

At first glance you might think she's some sort of throwback from the era of gel pens and tooth gems but this trope's new and hip (and chock full of fetish and fresh hell). Pop a Hello Kitty ribbon on her and she's the gift that keeps on giving.

THE CLUMSY COSPLAY OTAKU GIRL SCREAMS, SQUEAKS AND COY CHUCKLES

TRANSLATION:

'Hi! I'm the only Japanese girl in the gang!

My clothes and hair may be bright but I'm not. Someone mentioned shopping and my eyes bugged out of my head into heart shapes and toppled me over. If I'm not falling off my flatforms from a stationary position, I'm falling over myself!

I might be boring with a bassline of dumb but at least I'm here to replace the Japanese Tourist trope ... PROGRESS! ... HIGH FIVE!'

THE DAMSEL IN DISTRESS

An oldie but a goodie. We've been raised on them, we've been raised to BE them! Apart from creating her own brand of helplessness, she's so run of the mill and nondescript it's tricky to pin the damsel down but, NEVER FEAR — a man will be along to do so shortly.

Once upon a time, lost and alone in a wasteland of patriarchy, our time-honoured classic DAMSEL IN DISTRESS waited resignedly atop a tower for her knight in shining armour to show up.

The fair maiden's dismay leaked from her eyes as she daydreamed of becoming one of these 'Modern-Day Damsels in Distress'. The type that, despite centuries of chauvinism, have adapted to need rescuing from fixes as simple as being too weak to open jars instead.

How liberated women have become!

errrr...

THE DEADPAN SNARKER

You might think this trope has some promise — she gets to make every interaction an insult, hydrates on haterade and even belittles the boys! But you have to be a boff to snark and boffs are booger fugly. The snark is so deadpan she may as well BE dead.

EXT. BUS STOP. DAY

THE DEADPAN SNARKER waits for a bus. Her
life blows so much she should be having an
existential crisis but she's too busy being
obnoxious to care. This snarky-mc-snarkerson
is not good-looking and should be overjoyed
that a HUNK stops and brings himself to talk
to her.

HUNK:
Sorry, have you got the time?

DEADPAN SNARKER:
* Insert sarcastic slam here *

HUNK:
Okaaay. Any idea how long the wait for the
219 is then?

DEADPAN SNARKER:
* Insert witty comeback here *

HUNK (ALL-KNOWING, SING-SONGY VOICE):
What's his name ...?

DEADPAN SNARKER:
* Side eye *

HUNK:
Some guy must have made you this way.

DEADPAN SNARKER:
* Insert quirky and obscure literary
reference here *

HUNK:
Give me his address and I'll see to him
for you!

DEADPAN SNARKER:
* Death stare *

HUNK:
You're a fiery one, aren't you?

DEADPAN SNARKER:
* Slow, disdainful headshake *

HUNK:
Riiight. Well, here's the bus. I'm going
to come and sit next to you when we get on
(even though it's empty). Let's out-snark
each other for the entire journey until
our belligerent sexual tension becomes
a relationship!

DEADPAN SNARKER:
* Insert realisation that she's not deadpan,
actually, she's EXASPERATED, here *

END.

THE DECORATIVE BOLLYWOOD BOO

Pretty props are capable of launching into musical numbers underneath waterfalls too! But who cares for * actual talent * when she can set the scene with all the come-hither dexterity of her onscreen counterpart, THE SEDUCTIVE DOORMAT? Priceless entertainment!

Good morning class. Today's topic is...

'Strong female leads may be on the rise but are we still seeing THE DECORATIVE BOLLYWOOD BOO in disguise?' Discuss.

WAAAAIT A MINUTE ...

I didn't know we had a chaise longue?

... Woops! My bad. It's THE DECORATIVE BOLLYWOOD BOO (who appears to have commissioned her own personal hair-beautifying breeze) reclining melodramatically, dressing the set with her striking symmetry and lip-syncing herself into another realm in my peripheral.

Class dismissed.

THE DISABLED LOVE INTEREST

The hero will fancy a female who's worth the chirpse, but he'll soon discover that she's not because (shock, horror) she's DISABLED! He needs to grow and mature and she'll have to coach him through that. She's not good for much else so it's a relief for everyone to be fair.

GET YOUR BOGOF DISABLED TROPE BARGAIN TODAY*

PRICE SLASH!
MEGA SALE!
SPECIAL OFFER!
2 FOR THE
PRICE OF 1!

FREE
'INSPIRATIONALLY DISABLED' TROPE WHEN YOU BUY A 'DISABLED LOVE INTEREST' TROPE

FOR A LIMITED TIME ONLY

*Terms and conditions apply. Often the two are rolled into one and therefore you will only receive one trope. Tropes will have either been involved in a far-fetched accident or be inexplicably terminally ill. We cannot guarantee a realistic backstory or identity. Our only promise to you is that our tropes will speak profoundly, make others nod and soul-search and help male leads become half-decent human beings. Colours, shapes and defects may vary. We do our best to ensure that our descriptions of disabled characters are complete, accurate and current. Despite our best efforts, however, our descriptions of disabled characters may occasionally be incomplete, inaccurate and thoroughly out of date.

THE DISTURBED CHILD

This little one isn't made of sugar and spice (or anything nice at all, in fact). You could try and encourage her to do 'girl' hobbies like ballet or baking but this whackjob's more suited to throwing faeces, upchucking bile and lurking around corners.

TEXTBOOK ANXIETY DREAM (FEAT. THE DISTURBED CHILD)

You're naked. In public. You're late. Cue death rattle sound. All at once you're trapped in an attic and a little girl, so broken she needs to be put in rice, scuttles between the beams. Through the cobwebs you can just about make out that her eyes are wide (and spinning), her arms are outstretched and BLEEEEUUUURRRRGGGHH she's projectile vomited across the pile of dead-eyed dolls and right into your mouth.

You're at a playground somehow. This is a safe space now. THE DISTURBED CHILD is smiling and wearing pigtails. *Trigger warning* You can't just put cute bows on mental illness! She makes you chase her into a tunnel and you lose her. You hear her gently singing a nursery rhyme in the distance ... the reddest of red flags!

Now you're completely alone in a big white room. There are no doors, no windows, no escape. Behind you, a sinister snicker breaks the silence. Followed by another. SOMEONE ELSE ...

THE DISTURBED CHILD has an identical twin sister. You're no longer dreaming, you're dead.

Rest in peace.

THE EASTERN EUROPEAN CLEANER

She works 24/7 but also manages to somehow be a sponge on society. She's an ill-educated moron and yet she can crack codes on safes that could survive nuclear blasts. She smokes too much and exists too much — the type to outstay her welcome at a party (and in the country).

WANTED
CLEANER TO MOP MY FABULOUS FLOORS

Preferably an EASTERN EUROPEAN CLEANER so I can pay you abysmally. Polish / Ukrainian / Estonian? I don't care for specifics (no doubt you'll make every word plural for no reason anyway).

There will be no negotiation when it comes to hours or fee - most female tropes aren't allowed jobs full stop so you should count yourself lucky.

That said, I've seen your kind in domestic dramas, if I find you rifling through my jewellery box or polishing off my husband instead of polishing my home, I'll call immigration.

Phone me, but make sure to speak slowly. Whatever your name is, we will call you Olga. I look forward to saving you from being trafficked.

THE ENGLISH ROSE

Rose* (the woman of your mildest dreams) and her whoopee cushion pink cheeks should have cowered into a bin years ago, when the country that her purity is supposed to personify set itself on fire. Nevertheless, her meek manners and feeble temperament persisted!

The À La Mode English Rose Maketh Nay Sense!

Her iPhone 'twas tenderly sweet before her eyes,
held soft betwixt her lap.
Our ENGLISH ROSE forgot not her place
And ignored the dick pic Snap.

Rose had invite to playeth the harp
(And an ENGLISH ROSE need ne'er neglect her fate)
Rose's polyamorous pansexual meet-up
did belike need wait.

Shouldst she fight 'gainst her country, her lineage and go?
The patriarchy might forsooth falleth if 't be true so!
... But the real world 'twas a mere phone tappeth hence,
Rose hads't a rape alarm and kneweth self-defence!

Harping for gentle courtiers didst not compare a career,
Rose 'twas eager to Crowdfund her own tech start-up idea!
The mistress is a Millennial, this lifestyle was laughable
Wherefore shouldst the lady sew tapestry and be affable?

Fie! A gold ring shall prithee most any wench but Rose would rather die,
A 'Fries before Guys' T-shirt dress on ASOS she's espied!
The ENGLISH ROSE standards vexed and gallowed, Rose wenteth insane
She ripped off her Handmaid's bonnet and puffed on her Vape,
'F*CK IT!' she exclaimed.

*THE ENGLISH ROSE is often called Rose because: LAZINESS

THE EXOTIC FANTASY

She's fresh off the boat and she WANTS IT. Once the hero bulldozes in, she'll get it! You'll find her in 'traditional' costume: barely-there-swimwear or batty riders. Her personality is being cellulite- and jiggle-free and she'll show it off by throwing her legs around burly man-waists.

CASTING CALL

EXOTIC FANTASY (Name not relevant).
Female / 15-18 years (NOT A DAY OLDER) / 'Foreign looking' (any colour other than white).

Actress required to be a young, absolutely banging, walking pair of breasts. The plot has more holes than a loofah but THE EXOTIC FANTASY is a male gaze requirement. Only the poreless, pubeless, clueless and braless need apply.

Actress to prepare: In a sex-game gone wrong, THE EXOTIC FANTASY will be bludgeoned to death with a pitchfork in the shower. We will improvise the sex section.

Fee: Exposure.

THE FAT GIRL

In the wildfire of body politics, she might get burnt the most but thankfully she can binge eat her feelings away! Large but never in charge, she has to become the comic relief to prevent innocent bystanders becoming suicidal. Never make her hangry or look her in the eye (eugh).

HOW TO BECOME THE FAT GIRL in 15 easy steps:

1. You need only be a size bigger than minus zero. Follow your heart – to the fridge.
2. Allow yourself to become the butt of the joke. Literally.
3. Do nothing to dismantle fatphobia by straddling pizzas at any given opportunity.
4. Make the whale your spirit animal (beached).
5. Concede to be summoned by KFC family buckets in the centre of salt circles.
6. Fill clothes to capacity.
7. Break chairs, clear swimming pools and rooms.
8. Only do squats to get snacks out of vending machines.
9. Smile when FAT you are constantly reminded FAT that you FAT are FAT.
10. Decipher your nickname by putting the word FAT in front of your own name.
11. Only learn jokes that revolve around your weight. You need to be funny to survive.
12. Self-medicate with buffets. Self-medicate so hard that the body positivity movement gets lost among your rolls.
13. Know that if you are gifted any plot, it will be steered solely by your love handles.
14. Understand that you are not wifeable (but you stand a chance if your love interest gets a bump to the head and forgets their odious bias).
15. Get over the fact that your male equivalent will be cuddly, lovable (and 100% husbandable).

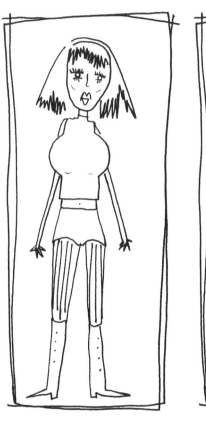

FEMBOT

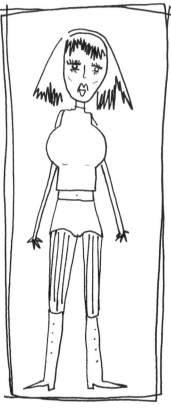

SEX ROBOT

THE FEMBOT

She's smouldering, sultry, sex on legs / wheels / runners / rudders. Honestly! What man wouldn't prefer a robo-romance? It's been a hard edit to ensure there aren't more bots than minority groups in this book (despite that feeling like an accurate representation of the landscape).

You might be forgiven for confusing THE FEMBOT with a 'sex robot' but they're COMPLETELY different! Check it out ...

★ Intellectually about as much use as the Microsoft Office 97 paperclip assistant
★ Moulded-on lady lumps
★ Luscious locks
★ Booty shorts so tight they make her bum hungry
★ To conclude ... an entirely submissive cock pocket!

THE FEMME FATALE

Her main trick is viciously slaying men, so try not to fall for that one — it's all she's really capable of, so you shouldn't miss it coming. Everything she does and says is a tripwire and she'll have blokes falling at her feet in a hot second. A woman to ACTUALLY die for.

As she lingers alluringly in the shadows,
sucking cigarettes through lipsticked smackers,
our FEMME FATALE awaits another witless
turd of a man on whom she will pounce and
emotionally bankrupt.

But how will she pass the time?

FEMME FATALE wonders if she could ever pursue
a hobby besides ensnaring men with her
feminine wiles?

She's quite taken by the idea of basket weaving
but that requires secateurs ... and she can't be
trusted with sharp objects ...

THE FINAL GIRL

This cutie patootie teenager (or, should we say, 30-year-old playing a teenager because 30-year-olds are more likely to have bigger boobs) is about to be the last woman in the story standing / writhing around half-naked on the floor. What larks!

INT. ABANDONED HOUSE IN THE WOODS. DEAD OF NIGHT

Blam! Blam! Blam! The FINAL GIRL's best friends (the BEAUTY QUEEN, the JOCK and the 'ETHNICALLY AMBIGUOUS' BORE) die bloodcurdling deaths at the hands of the killer in a murder montage.

CUT TO:

CU of the FINAL GIRL. Her clothes have been shredded. She's left without even her v-plates to cover her modesty (her hair and makeup, however, are still magnifleek). She hides in a cupboard, covered in blood, panting orgasmically and clutching a phallic-y weapon.

GENERIC HORROR VOICE-OVER GUY:
All her friends are dead, the Killer has pushed THE FINAL GIRL to the edge! But THE FINAL GIRL has a boyishness about her that re-genders her

enough for her survival skills to make sense.
Perhaps she will fashion a flame thrower out of a
scrunchie or hotwire a car using nothing but a
potato peeler? She's extraordinarily able (for
a girl!).

The FINAL GIRL crosses her chest, raises her
weapon and lurches out of the darkness with a
warlike battle cry.

FADE TO BLACK.

GENERIC HORROR VOICE-OVER
GUY:
(Ts&Cs VOICE) THE FINAL
GIRL contains
objectification,
violence towards
women, rape and
torture. Not
suitable for
children, pets,
the faint-hearted
or feminists.

END.

THE FISH OUT OF WATER

She won't know how to blink or put one foot in front of the other but she can swiftly introduce you to the end of your tether. She's as daft as a box of toads and out to crumble your Zen. Anything can break this delicate wee dear and usually does. Bring Kleenex (and a shotgun).

HOW TO SAVE A FISH OUT OF WATER:

1. Firstly, you must decipher if she's been grown in a lab or if this is a woman who (for no goddam reason) doesn't know how to act normally. Check for gills and flippers / limbs.
2. She can't grasp how to use a knife and fork but she could deliver a masterclass in missing the point. Be patient – she's an idiot.
3. Whatever danger THE FISH OUT OF WATER might be in, it could be avoided if she did something, rather than yelp aimlessly. Issue a muzzle.
4. It will be impossible to determine her natural habitat but she certainly won't have come from an academic environment. Talk at her slowly and loudly.
5. Assign her to a man as quickly as possible to get her out of this horrid predicament.
6. THE FISH OUT OF WATER can't walk but she can swoon – ensure to give her enough space to fall at the feet of said saviour.

THE FIT AMAZONIAN WITH THE SWORD

The sword is hardly worth a mention — it's her features rather than the fighting that bring all the boys to her yard. She'll be easy on the eyes for the audience and the hero ... who we're all here for anyhow! (Why is anyone bothering to mention the female lead?)

FAN SERVICE. DIRECTOR'S NOTES:

* x6 shots of FIT AMAZONIAN thumping men because she's 'empowered' (but the focus should be on her bouncy boobs and blow dry*).
* Minimum x4 close ups of her ass in hot pants as she cartwheels her way into the part of the plot where the hero saves her.
* x1 slow mo of her sword wielding (insecurely). Perhaps a tight on a teardrop splashing onto the shaft?
* FIT AMAZONIANS still need super feminine moments too (flowers in hair?).
* More smizing and lip licking.
* Ramp up the sex in every scene. Even the one where her father dies.
* PENIS-PUMPING MOMENTS OVER PLOT.

*There's a new runner who keeps tutting every time we go for a take and questioning where THE FIT AMAZONIAN WITH A SWORD would get her hair done in the middle of the rainforest. Fire her. (Political correctness gone mad.)

THE FUNNY BFF

Whatever her background, this gal is used to standing on the sidelines, hanging on the coat-tails of her practically perfect-in-every-way best mate. She sometimes gets yanked into her makeover montages, but she's too quick-witted and smart to be anything other than repugnant.

THE FATE OF THE FUNNY BFF (IN A NUTSHELL*):

... SHE'S ALWAYS THE BRIDESMAID, NEVER THE BRIDE!

*(and you best believe she'll make jokes about being trapped inside a nutshell / death by nut allergy / being the 'nutty' one!)

THE GIRL NEXT DOOR

A real brain drain. She may be a main character but she'll never be important. Her duty is to be the male hero's backscratcher, punchbag, subordinate and biggest fan. Don't invite her anywhere — she's cleared her diary to allow time for her 'meet cute' moment.

INNER MONOLOGUE:

I could get bangs cut in?
(Maybe not.)
I'm just so dainty!
Should I take a photo of myself laughing at salad?
(I'd rather be snot-sobbing into a tube of Pringles.)
I'm just so unassuming!
Maybe if I sell my Beanie Baby collection I'd become a millionaire?
(But, like, what's the point when I inexplicably live in this million-pound apartment?)
I'm just so wholesome!
Where's my brown paper bag of groceries?
(I haven't watched my apples roll all over the street in distress yet today.)
I'm just so pretty but accessible!
I wonder why I'm always falling into men's arms?
(I better get checked for early onset Type 2 diabetes.)
I'm just so sweet and ordinary!
... It's strange that everyone calls me THE GIRL NEXT DOOR, but I have no neighbours.

THE GOOD GIRL GONE BAD

Perhaps she started life as THE ENGLISH ROSE or THE GIRL NEXT DOOR, but life took a turn — a bad turn. She's a hot-mess product of her own atrocious life choices; a sexed-up, multi-vehicle car crash explosion. THE GOOD GIRL GONE BAD is exactly as she says on the tin and worse.

An unexplained trauma has stripped her of all humility and clothing!

No longer a dullard, THE GOOD GIRL GONE BAD has become a raging dong demon overnight!

THE GORGEOUS GLUTTON

Turns out that women aren't livid at the state of the world, they're just low on blood sugar! Who knew?! There are stick insect-thin women out there who can polish off a sharer double dozen of Krispy Kremes and never need negotiate a Zumba Merengue March. Bonkers!

UNPOPULAR OPINION: THE GORGEOUS GLUTTON EDITION

Attractive women are allowed to eat!

THE GRANOLA GIRL

The world has moved on from hippies, beatniks and bohemians — a snowflake storm blew in and birthed GRANOLA GIRL! Like the second day of a hangover that won't give up or a 5 a.m. alarm without a snooze option, she won't rest until she can freely mourn her imagined oppression.

THE CONTENTS OF GRANOLA GIRL'S (VEGAN) HANDBAG:

★ 1kg of organic chia seeds (even walking, talking chickpeas need to snack).

★ A cluster of healing crystals.

★ Draft one of her think-piece on how therapy cured her therapy addiction.

★ A Post-It note reminding her to breathe.

★ x3 solid shampoo bars that smell like spunk and disappointment.

★ A combined meditation, dream and gratitude journal.

★ Lip balm in a 'namaste' tin.

★ x96 rogue hair pins.

★ A leaflet for a navel-gazing workshop.

THE HAPPY HOUSEWIFE

Happily married is an understatement, this woman's ECSTATICALLY married! She might not be able to do up the back of her dress, but she always manages to fix her husband's tie without fashioning it into a noose! She's a goddess and her children are angels. Domestic BLISS.

THE HAPPY COUPLE: A COMPARATIVE ANALYSIS

	WIFE	HUSBAND
PERSONALITY	A flannel	N/A (never around long enough to decipher)
APPEARANCE	Wears whatever keeps hubby pleased in the pants	Wears whatever THE HAPPY HOUSEWIFE irons and presses for him
PARENTING ABILITY	Delighted to do EVERYTHING for her children with constant boom-banging levels of excitement (verging on heart attack concerns)	Gracious enough to never complain that his wife runs around tirelessly after his kids whilst he is forced to go out and have all the fun
APPETITE	No time to eat (as she has to prepare a Henry VIII-style breakfast feast at the buttcrack of dawn every morning)	Ignores the magnificent spread and runs out of the door snaffling a bite of toast as THE HAPPY HOUSEWIFE finishes dressing him
MENTAL STABILITY	Questionable but don't be too alarmed if you find her with her head in the oven – she'll probably only be deep cleaning it	Sometimes he drapes a tea towel over his shoulder for no reason when he's in the kitchen vicinity (but otherwise balanced and brilliant)

THE HARDENED DETECTIVE

She refuses to solve crimes until she's made a mood board on the matter. She's lonely, she's cynical, she's probably got OCD and she never gets invited to the staff party. But she couldn't be powerful AND problem-free! Women with agency have to be flawed victims.

EVIDENCE TO PROVE (BEYOND ALL REASONABLE DOUBT) THAT THE DETECTIVE IS HARDENED:

★ She was caught on CCTV narrowing her eyes, staring into the middle distance, agonising over where the killer is and shout-whispering about it.

★ Eyewitnesses saw her handling stones, leaving not one unturned.

★ Hours of recordings have been made of her effing and jeffing.

★ Photographs of the detective with a female colleague capture her inability to work alongside other women without strangling them.

★ DNA results determine that she smokes approximately eighty-five rollies a day and swigs hard liquor at her desk.

★ An office inspection verified that she can't solve cases unless she tapes all of the evidence to the walls and links clues together with pins and red string.

★ In an official statement, a trainee constable on the force described her as 'the human form of sitting on a wet public toilet seat'.

★ Another said that getting on the wrong side of her was as 'risky as sneezing on your period'.

★ The forensics team say that her hands have been superglued into the steeple position.

★ She's seen it all and done it all so, *naturally*, she's a psycho.

THE HOT SCIENTIST

She probably only got into science because she used to let her high school biology teacher pound her over the dissection table! The overall 'watch out' here is to be cautious of any female with a hint of clever clogs or spark of live wire — they're bound to throw a hissy fit soon ...

Dear HOT SCIENTIST,

This letter is to confirm that your employment with us is terminated, effective immediately.

We've been observing your behaviour for the past three months and have come to this decision after deliberating the following points:

- You never use safety glasses or gloves and allow your hair to tousle and tumble over bunsen burners.
- You have motivational spurts to find treatments for incurable diseases, but park them the second a man enters the lab.
- You've changed all of the lighting fixtures without our permission so you can work in the sexy glow of a dimmer.
- You clearly have terrible interpersonal skills – nobody ever listens to you until it's too late.
- You pretend to be interested in angular momentum quantum, molecular geometry, finding cures for cancer (and the like) and yet you only ever stand about squeezing the same pipette.
- You should be inspirational but, in fact, you're aggravating.

It has also come to our attention that nobody as young as you could have possibly completed a PhD.

We thank you for your service and wish it didn't have to end this way. We will miss your gaping lab coat cleavage and calling you 'Test Tube Totty' behind your back. In the long run, we are certain the best decision has been made here – perhaps you can settle down and start a family now instead.

Regrettably,

Your (genius-man-scientist) Superior

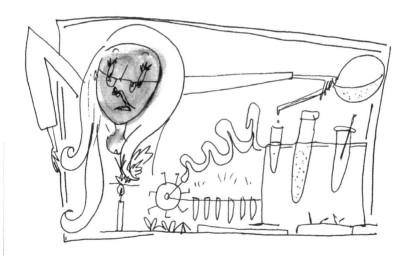

THE IRON LADY

In the biggest turn-up for the trope book, this one has wangled a way to own a vulva AND be a boss! You'll know your place when you meet her because she'll put you in it. Imposter Syndrome? She's never heard of it! ... Or has she?

ATTENBOROUGH-ESQUE PROLOGUE:

And here we have a very rare sighting indeed – a middle-aged woman. This Extremius Bitchidus (or IRON LADY), to you and I, is a world-weary battleaxe who turns Snow Queens to Slush Puppies. The more astute trope-spotters among you will know that nothing interesting happens to women in this final chapter of their lives (unless a husband leaves or buries them). She's a man hater not because of her powerhouse leadership qualities but because a man dumped her when her showbiz shelf-life expired.

IRON LADIES are aloof. Asexual and power-jacketed. Masculine. A true wonder to behold ... see how she skulks about! She can't run in case she slips and falls on her own sense of entitlement.

Approach the Bitchidus at your peril, but know that people struggle to get anywhere near her. The mating habits of this species are similarly non-existent. If you are very patient you *might* catch her smiling ... but only in the most sombre hours of the morning, when she thinks nobody can see her crack ...

THE LIPSTICK LESBIAN

She likes lipstick, ladies and putting gay rights progress to shame! So femme she's (confusingly) more magnetic than the straight girls — who she'll 'turn lesbian' anyway! A woman so fantasised over and well documented, it's frankly embarrassing that we're giving her any more airtime.

INT. NIGHTCLUB. MIDNIGHT

THE LIPSTICK LESBIAN kisses her lipstick lover, discreetly but passionately on the dancefloor. Instantaneously, the eyes of every man in the place are on the pair. DOUCHEBAGUETTE approaches the couple.

DOUCHEBAGUETTE:
Girl on girl? Hot! Can i join in?

LIPSTICK LESBIAN & HER LOVER:
Hell yeah! We're blouse unbuttoning, skirt dropping, finger sucking, hyper-feminine, jiz hungry jez's!

LIPSTICK LESBIAN:
We've been waiting for you to ask us all night!

DOUCHEBAGUETTE:
I knew this was all for me!

LIPSTICK LESBIAN:
Too right! This is just a phase! Now take me.
Quickly! Show me what I've been missing.

THE LIPSTICK LESBIAN's lover undoes
DOUCHEBAGUETTE's pants and gets him going whilst
he strips THE LIPSTICK LESBIAN and ravishes
her with his clumsy, furry tongue. The girls
go back to kissing each other but lock eyes
with DOUCHEBAGUETTE, inviting him back into the
crotch party. He accepts and the women's moans
grow louder than the music in the club.
DOUCHEBAGUETTE looks directly down the barrel
with entitlement and alpha eyebrows, as the
girls simultaneously climax.

END.

THE MANIC PIXIE DREAMGIRL

This mad head is barmy for adventure and she's here to give our hero a rollicking good time! Her energy is boundless and as childlike as her body. She says 'nom nom' when she eats and hums show tunes in the street. She's easy and easily pleased – just give her a pack of Crayola!

STORYTIME!

THE DAY THE MANIC PIXIE DREAMGIRL CAUGHT ON TO FINGER GUNS

After taking a wrong turn out of Narnia one morning, our kooky, brain glitchy MANIC PIXIE DREAMGIRL felt all panic and no disco. She was terribly lost! She wished she'd stayed home, listened to some pseudo self-help podcasts and made cupcakes. How could she share her disease to please with others now? There wasn't a single square bear male in sight who she could teach to roller-skate or save from his own pathetic lack of charisma.

THE MANIC PIXIE DREAMGIRL was bewildered and unarmed (especially as she hadn't packed her trusty ukulele or Lomography camera in her neon knapsack). Truly, she didn't know whether to drop and roll or perform an avant-garde mime drama to interpret her emotions.

BUT THEN, as true as a unicorn's blood runs rainbow, rather than single-handedly keep the anxiety economy afloat, THE MANIC PIXIE DREAMGIRL knew what she had to do to survive – WACKY HIJINKS! She skipped, swung her arms around a bit, did a little knee bend dance and attempted to create a whimsical farmyard shadow puppet show with her bare hands (but the sun had gone in). Fiddling with her fingers reminded her of an excruciatingly ironic yet ha-ha-larious gesture she flipped out over once. She decided to try it on for size.

POW! POW!

And just like that she was back in her skin. Finger guns fit THE MANIC PIXIE DREAMGIRL like a dream!

THE MISTRESS

This wretched woman will be vilified more than her man, even if he's a locker-room banterer with a girl in every postcode. She won't rest until she's visited all of the weekend-break hotels in the country and given his children mental health jip for life.

She'll snake on your life and bag your man,
Getting chummy with his money is her only plan.
Distracting married men so they forget they're wed,
THE MISTRESS cuffs 'em quick and scams 'em into bed.
Victims might be more desirable if they still use roman numerals,
These gold diggers are well versed in catching bouquets at funerals.
Perhaps the husband made all the moves with *her*?
(There'll likely even be witnesses.)
But it will NEVER be the Lothario's fault,
IT'S ONLY EVER THE MISTRESS'S!

THE MURDEROUS BISEXUAL

Narratively useless (because the sexuality spectrum isn't a thing and therefore these so-called 'bisexuals' are baffling!). She'll make the most of her precious moment in the spotlight by destroying your man or woman. She's not picky (but she is damaged and attention seeking).

PSYCHOTHERAPIST'S NOTES – AREAS OF CONCERN:

* She is a former goth on the edge of a relapse (high risk).
* The patient bemoans the fact she keeps seeing shrinks but her problems have never shrunk (delusional).
* Hates having to rattle off her romantic history to prove herself but is similarly proud of her conquests (cognitive dissonance).
* She tried to sales pitch me an all-inclusive trip to the abyss (projection).
* Hypersexual to the point of crushing on herself naked (narcissist).
* Believes it normal to dream of 'taking [my] eyeballs, then returning for the sockets' (disassociation).
* Refuses to pick a side or explain why she is only ever seen to have relations with people of the same sex (defensive).
* Her name says it all (self-fulfilling prophecy).

Case summary: THE MURDEROUS BISEXUAL is untreatable.

THE MUSLIM TERRORIST

Obscene headline hatred and Islamophobic caricatures have proved time and time again that there's only one type of Muslim woman in this world — dressed in black from head to toe and a threat! She won't have the brain capacity to be brainwashed — she's following hubby's orders ...

'Welcome back to THE OPPRESSION OLYMPICS!

(We apologise for the unplanned break in this programme but our security was breached by a group of Caucasian, male, far-right extremists, who, claiming Terrorist Attack Top Trumps, tried to steal the winner's trophy for themselves.)

But now, without further ado, we can finally announce ...
In first place for the *nineteenth consecutive year (since September 2001 ...)*

Always veiled! Always oppressed! And usually bedecked in an explosive vest!

It'sssss ... THE MUSLIM TERRORIST!'

THE MUTE

Not only can she not speak but — UH OH! — She seems to have caught the stupids too! Whatever has rendered her speechless has also made her a guileless liability. Is she really mute or have the writers forgotten that whimpers don't equate to dialogue? She can't say. Because she's MUTE.

She might be as depress-fest as the bit between Christmas and New Year ... but at least you'll never have to tell her to *SHADDAP!*

She's the star of men's liquid dreams: THE MUTE!

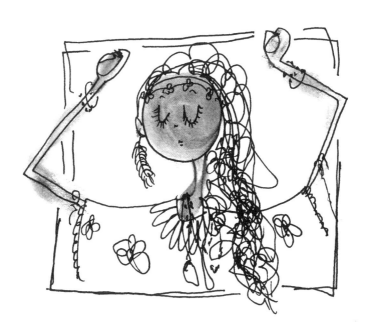

THE MYSTICAL WAIF

This fruitcake could do with a lot more naps and snacks. If you were avoiding the problem you might say she was a bit 'nervy'. She's unnatural because she has a brain and uses it to selflessly guide men to safety. More terrifying than urinating and forgetting you've had beetroot.

SPOT THE MYSTICAL WAIF!

CLUES:

1. She's as thin as a hair and flakier than psoriasis.
2. Social skills she does not possess, but magical plot-navigating powers she might.
3. Prone to floating on cloud ten one minute and drowning in shallow lakes to classical music the next.
4. She's a recreational witchcraft fan (particular penchant for curses).
5. If the hero is lost THE MYSTICAL WAIF will catch him, she will be waiting, time after time.

she's behind the weeping willow tree

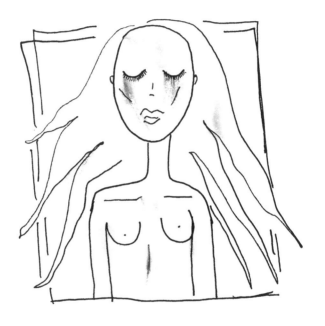

THE NAKED AND NAMELESS CORPSE

A high percentage of victims freeze and stay silent when being attacked. This girl has taken both ideas to the extreme. She's on ice, she's voiceless and yet her contouring is on point. Her only job is to flaunt the normalcy of female victimhood and she's excelling in her role. Enjoy!

EPIC TRAILER VOICE-OVER GUY:

She's naked, she's nameless, she's ... she's a ... who is she? Nobody cares because we're not here to sit and watch dexterous, intriguing women tell their significant life stories! We're here to watch them serve the plot and kicks of men!

THE NAKED AND NAMELESS CORPSE may be in an industrial freezer but she's still insanely hot!

THE NAKED AND NAMELESS CORPSE ... coming soon to a cinema near you (for approximately 15 seconds of screen time).

(THE NAKED AND NAMELESS CORPSE does not contain content warnings because they are spoilers that ruin the thrill of brutal details. We've already told you she's a corpse! What more is there to say?! That's why this trailer can be short and entirely uneventful ... just like her life!)

THE NOLLYWOOD HOUSEWIFE

This poor love doesn't get out much. Has anyone checked on her recently to make sure she's ok? If she's not looking for a husband, she's wishing she could leave one or scheming to steal one. She cooks, cleans and lives to provide. To top it all off, she's also an object of barter!

'It's with *cough* sincere pleasure *cough* I welcome you to my kitchen and officially declare it the *cough* supposed *cough*

... BEST PLACE FOR A NOLLYWOOD HOUSEWIFE TO BE!'

THE PARTY GIRL

This absolute sex biscuit likes short skirts, strong drinks and is prone to logic wobbles and intelligence flatlining. Give her a few years and she may become one of the tropes we don't have the word count or energy to unpack — the ultimate amusement — The Alcoholic!

She'd rather shot tequila from her Mooncup than consider
    sexual abstention,
THE PARTY GIRL is long overdue a staged intervention.
Some call it 'Stag Do Behaviour' but she calls it weekend (and
    weeknight) fun,
THE PARTY GIRL only gets LADS! LADS! LADS! when mixed
    with rum.
She'd attend the opening of a septic wound, this one's at all
    the bashes,
THE PARTY GIRL marks her territory with hair extensions and
    fake lashes.
Chewing tonsils, throwing shapes, having a 'cheeky' dry heave,
THE PARTY GIRL's gums and nostrils are demanding annual leave.
She'll never admit to falling off the wagon, despite being dragged
    alongside one,
THE PARTY GIRL can dance all night in heels though (Still got it!
    Still a DON).
Always the last one standing, sometimes the last one slumped,
THE PARTY GIRL will end up one of two ways: tamed by a man ...
    or bumped.

THE RACIST GRANDMA

Move over 'Old Hags' and 'Lovable Nans'! There's a racist OAP trope in town — and racism is still side-splitting AF! Some will reckon her comments are merely 'racially charged' or perhaps only slightly 'racially tinged' but, hilariously and preposterously, they'll be racists too!

THE RACIST GRANDMA is a racist. Other crimes include but aren't limited to:

★ Eternal idiocy.
★ Remorseless trolling.
★ Marrying a Nazi Grandpa.
★ Straight-shooting opinions that are more bespoke than woke.
★ Practising ball gown and black tie racism (never casual).
★ Believing herself to be open-minded.
★ Dragging around a heart full of ancient hatred.
★ Hollering cerebrum-melting nonsense that pops eardrums and burns retinas.
★ Having a sense of humour that will ruin her bloodline for generations.
★ Constantly pouring herself whisky rather than a nice refreshing glass of 'mind your own business'.

THE RUSSIAN VILLAIN

All Russians are evil criminals. Male villains definitely get to have more craic but the women are at least granted some wickedly tight suits and cackles! Conclusion jumpists might imagine this to be a harmless trope but she's a cliche so cliched she would make a mockery of pantomime.

Q: Why does THE RUSSIAN VILLAIN need to be Russian?

A: Bekauuse zey hav hilarrriously vicked karrrtoon accents, of kourrrse!

THE SASSY BLACK WOMAN

In the treasure trove of black woman tropes that exist only to be the white characters' support system, this trope is the prize booty! Although we were petrified of snubbing and riling THE ANGRY BLACK WOMAN, we couldn't not big up this crowd pleasing, mouthy, mainstream fave!

TO DO LIST:

Monday – Twerk.
Tuesday – Kiss teeth.
Wednesday – Grunt and neck roll.
Thursday – Finger snap and screech.
Friday – Flick weave and eat wings.
Saturday – Shake jelly at every chance.
Sunday (day off) – Relish my many nuances, complexities and contradictions. Luxuriate in my own intelligence, talents, sexuality and spiritual multidimensionality. Enjoy my myriad human emotions IN PEACE.

THE SPICY LATINA

It's a fact universally acknowledged that there are no ugly Latinas. She's had a rough childhood so she can fend for herself (but she won't have to once she is married!). In the meantime, she should book a fitting appointment at M&S because her bra keeps flying off without warning.

CHAT UP LINES USED TO BED THE SPICY LATINA (ALL SUCCESSFUL BECAUSE SHE EXISTS TO SEX MEN):

★ Hola, chica! You wanna live la vida loca with me?

★ What I wouldn't give to eat your taco, mamacita!

★ Marry me, baby! I can getchoo papers!

★ Yeesh! You're hotter than hot sauce on jalapeño!

★ You're giving me a fiesta in my pants!

★ Mami, you can roll your R's all over my enchilada any day of the week!

★ Oh, so you're a good Catholic girl? You look muy muy naughty to me!

★ I'm not like those other guys. I wouldn't beat you even if you were a piñata ...

THE STRUGGLING SINGLE MUM

When she's not stripping, she's shoplifting liquid eyeliner and nappies. Her kids are unruly, her bills are piling up and she drinks her way through the day. She kisses her (crackhead) mother with that mouth *and* all the boys' bits on the block. Because working class equals worthless.

THE TROPE AWARDS HOST:

'When I was first asked to present this award I was humbled, as I've had the pleasure of avoiding its recipient in the street for the last twenty-five years. Her shatteringly shameful existence finds her stuck beneath a class ceiling stained with nicotine and abuse, yet she succeeds at finding the means to make outstanding contributions to both the local offies and bookies.

'Her life is chaotic, her kids have jam around their mouths, she's so poor she has to eat sleep for dinner and quenches her thirst on faucet punch and bin-juice. Let us celebrate a woman who counts her blessings on one hand and should lay her last 'woe is me' to rest ... because tonight we're recognising her for once, instead of the null and void baby father.

'Please join me in raising a tinnie and a Turkey Twizzler in her honour ...

'The Lifetime of Scrounging Benefits Achievement award goes to ...

'... THE STRUGGLING SINGLE MUM!'

THE TOKEN ASIAN FRIEND

Every friendship group needs a miscellaneous Asian friend, right? Right! The perfect excuse for creatives to feel better about themselves and add more jokes about race, this Asian nobody is possibly a somebody — but deep diving into sensible human fundamentals is too much effort.

EMAIL TO: THE TOKEN ASIAN FRIEND
Subject: Fly tipping

Cc: The Kung Fu Fanatics, Karate Kids, Maths Experts, Hidden Dragons, Mafia Princesses, Fan Flickers, Kimono Kweens, Mail Order Brides & umpteen others

Dear TOKEN ASIAN FRIEND (and friends),

We are addressing this to all as it is impossible to say which interchangeable Asian character, from which interchangeable Asian country or culture, is responsible for the fly tipping of the ASIAN TROPE BANDWAGON.

Not only is the wagon an eyesore and criminal offence, it has become incredibly laden down. We have been patient with you as you have campaigned for sensitivity, narratives that give you a sniff of validation and for your incessant stereotyping to be labelled as a hate crime – but enough is enough.

We, the council, provide a comprehensive waste collection service and (although we take your point about the tropes being recyclable) we're afraid that we deal in white goods only.

Please contact us immediately if you no speak English,

Rubbish Management

THE TOMBOY

Women and girls would get catcalled wearing bin bags. If this young hoyden thinks she's going to escape objectification by stepping out in tracksuits, she's got another think coming! (It's also highly probable that she's a massive gay but if she finds her femininity soon she could be saved.)

LOST. HAVE YOU SEEN THIS TOMBOY?

Most likely to be found sport-loving, trouser-wearing or refusing to conform, this outdoorsy wreck is a threat to society norms.

She has five brothers, teeth resembling a zipper and smells like the mild funk of a teenager's plastic watch strap. A girl matching her description was spotted at the missing person's home address but it *couldn't possibly* have been her (she was wearing pink that day).

Anyone who sees THE TOMBOY is advised not to approach as she is a free-thinking, convention defying, proto-feminist with ambition. It's far too dangerous.

THE TRANS SEX WORKER

Trans women can't get normal jobs, they'd be laughed out of the job centre! She's a sex worker and addict because OF COURSE she is. Don't question the rules! Any opinions she might have would be a waste of lungs but we can be grateful that she's ~~ticking a box~~ being represented.

'THE TRANS SEX WORKER' DRAFT 1

INT. BEDSIT. EVENING.

The room is strewn with sex litter and drug paraphernelia and our taboo love interest (THE TRANS SEX WORKER) applies lipstick in slow motion, searching desperately for answers in every reflective surface. He She has been beaten and is badly bruised.

CUT TO:
Flashback of the night before. THE TRANS SEX WORKER is running for her life (in red stilletos), through an alleyway.

CUT BACK TO BEDSIT:
THE TRANS SEX WORKER has been shaken out of her PTSD memory by a thundering knock at the door. It's FANCY SUIT GUY. He's a guy, he's in a fancy suit and he's here to get to know THE TRANS SEX WORKER (find out if she has had bottom surgery or not and how much she charges!).

Note to editors: I can copy and paste her ending from any other script. Let's save time here and decide which cisgender male we should cast instead? Who do we know that would be disconcertingly womanish in a wig? ;-)

THE VIRGIN

She might be an **UNEXPECTED VIRGIN**, she might be the **SACRIFICED VIRGIN**, she might even be a **CHASTE HEROINE** but mark my words, that virginity will be roughly stolen from her by the end of play. And once she pops, she'll never want to stop!

★ Still in patent Mary Janes and bobby socks
★ Lives her life in U but daydreams in PG
★ Ready for a man mountain
★ Eyes welcoming your filthy paws on her silky drawers (they could be mistaken for 'I want sex' eyes even through acute conjunctivitis)
★ Gagging to get her pickle tickled
★ Mouth ready to orgasm the world down during white-hot sex (despite never indulging in any sort of 'self-discovery' to understand what she might actually enjoy)
★ Ripe and ready
★ Smells like teen spirit
★ Out of training bras (so she must be old enough!)
★ Waiting patiently to be made into a whore*

*You can only be a Virgin or a Whore. There's no middle ground.

THE WHORE

Our men need a break! All of this running around, saving the world, womanising in their sleep and being heroic must be EXHAUSTING! Thank fried Christ that this slag bag is waiting for them at the end of a long day's slog. Three cheers for THE WHORE!

INTRODUCTION TO SCRIPT:

We find THE WHORE bound and gagged and getting it because at some point in her life she's expressed a smidge of interest in her own sexuality (any woman who shows a diddle of dominance will undoubtedly be into nunchucking butt-plugs and trampling testicles in 12-inch stripper shoes too).

The camera pans across a boudoir floor full of tossed wholesale tubs of yoghurt (presumably used by THE WHORE to soothe her bits after sex-a-thons with football teams).

Cue moans of ravish.

Despite going like the clappers there's not a single bead of sweat on her body.

(Female characters are three times more likely to take their clothes off than their male counterparts and yet the whore defies all odds by being relentlessly starkers. It allows her to achieve the impossible – she need never fumble with a bra strap or wriggle free from a trouser leg. In fact, so beyond belief is THE WHORE she can achieve genuine orgasm through penetration alone!

THE WHORE isn't a trope. She's a groundbreaking pioneer and beacon for womanhood!)

END.